MW00810665

BITTER ANGELS

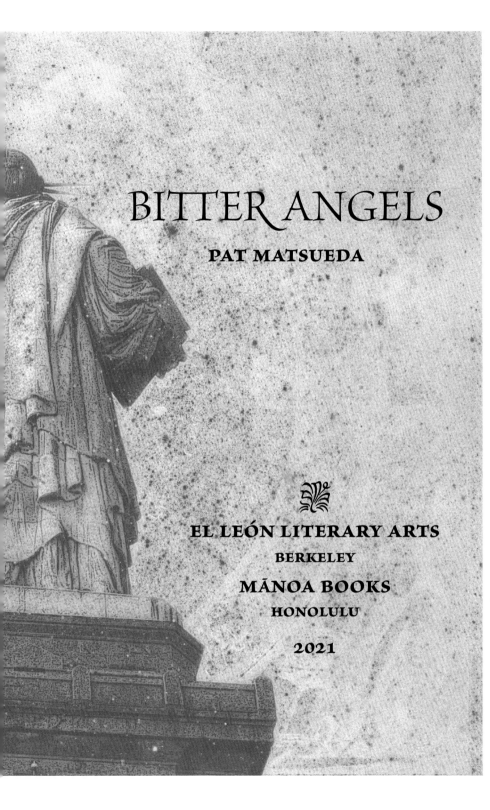

BITTER ANGELS

PAT MATSUEDA

EL LEÓN LITERARY ARTS

BERKELEY

MĀNOA BOOKS

HONOLULU

2021

Copyright 2021 Pat Matsueda

Published by

El León Literary Arts, of Berkeley, California
elleonliteraryarts.org

Mānoa Books
an imprint of Mānoa Foundation, of Honolulu, Hawaiʻi
manoafoundation.org

No part of this book may be reproduced in any manner
without written consent from the publishers, except in brief
quotations used in reviews of the book.

"My Friend Looks at the Horizon" and "Poem for My
Unborn Son" originally appeared in the second and third edi-
tions, respectively, of *Ms. Aligned: Women Writing About Men*.
"Valentine's Day" originally appeared in *Mānoa: A Pacific
Journal of International Writing*. The author thanks the editors
of these publications for their support.

ISBN 978-0-9799504-3-8
Printed in the United States of America

Designed by Peak Services (peakserviceshawaii.com)

Contents

for Kathleen Chiyo Matsueda
(1956–2020)

I shal deck your mynyon face
that yt shal shyne in euery place.

Songs of Anglia

Untitled Life

Shadows busy
as shadows are,
breaking light into
disks spinning out of trees
and landing at my feet

Moving, going
somewhere my feet
step on shadows and disks of light
world in motion
but step on nothing

Time busy
as time is
breaking my life into
thought, reflection, regret
       In the rush of experiences

we can't tell
the placid scene from the one
near the end—
the one that hurries at us
quietly

Engines in the Sky

In the summer of marches and protests
a reporter is blinded by a bullet to the eye
a woman is kicked in the face
a child is tear-gassed and
a man is shoved backward,
cracking his head on concrete
Blood flows from his ear
and pours on the ground

Gods of oppression, fury, and ignorance fight,
filling the sky with fire
with the lash of metal on bone and skull
In the night, copters hover in "persistent presence"
and rotary blades churn a power
that whips small trees,
sucks dirt and debris into the sky

The people crane their necks
at the sinister machines:
what force put engines in the sky
what force made them menace the people
The country drags down the brave who stand

Guardian

You are always addressing the transcendent mystery
through the conditions of your actual world.
Joseph Campbell

Her old face breaking through the thick layer of makeup,
her long hair dyed black and braided,
the Hawaiian woman leaves her seat by the wall
and approaches the long table regally,
then sits and speaks when
the young man asks for further testimony.
The legislative body is to decide who
shall study violence in the home.

"I come here," she says slowly,
"to share my expertise.
My husband beat me, and I
and my ten children suffered.
Later, I was arrested for trespassing
and taken to court.
People wanted to put me in an insane asylum.
I realized it was
because I was to inherit the throne
that I was suffering.
Pele wishes to cleanse the world with fire,
but I choose to save it another way."

On three resolutions she speaks,
the last time saying only,
"I come here to share my expertise"
when the young man hits the table with his gavel.
She stops, confused. Her gaze
slides up the wall to the fluorescent lights,
then falls.
Her large figure rises slowly and she resumes her seat,
obedient to the strike.
Two women quietly walk up to her,
pay homage with soft words and kisses on the cheek.
She then leaves, but before passing through the door,
she turns and bows slightly,
her eyes wide,
lined thickly so they make their arrest,
her full muʹumuʹu a sheen of pinks
and on her shoulders a mantle of gold lace.
She stares in innocence down the long corridor
her pain has carved through the world.

II HER SOLILOQUY

*If mystery is manifest through all things, the
universe becomes, as it were, a holy picture.*
Joseph Campbell

When my sister passed away, I became queen.
I inherited the throne
upon which God laid our suffering.

This suffering was great because
our glory was to endure.
My daughter speaks to the governors now,
tells them of her birthright.
"Your laws do not bind me," she says,
"a half-blooded indigenous aborigine.
Why do the courts wish to take my children away?
We have the wisdom to raise them ourselves;
let our elders be our leaders.
We have a place of refuge;
let us be free to go there."
How well she speaks, my daughter.
The power is in her.

Pele wishes to save the world with fire,
but I choose to enlighten it.
Violence destroyed my mortal self
and suffering made me a queen.
The universe, once a holy vessel,
is shattered now.
Every creature lifts its tiny fragment
over its head.
Yes, everything carries
the broken image of its queen.

Naming the Angels

1

Her father tried to break her spirit
By beating her flesh
He subdued the angel that said
She was the breath of heaven
Fallen on Earth

How the light found her
And lifted her out of the dark place
Where she had gone to die
Is a story in the language of family:
Tears, blood, secret scars

2

Baby Hope was found in a cooler
Abandoned in a park
When the caretaker opened it
Drawn by the smell,
An arm fell out, the fingers closed
As if grasping the ladder to heaven

For decades her rape and murder
Remained a mystery
Police drove slowly down the streets
Blaring a question through their loudspeakers:
Who is she?

Then a woman remembered
A conversation in a laundromat years before:
Someone mentioned her brother
Had killed a child
It was they who carried the cooler to the park
Baby Hope's uncle is tried, convicted
And we learn her christened name:
Angelique, spun from the gold of clouds

3

The man, a writer—
And other writers perhaps—
Tells a story:
Chaste, we must learn sin;
Innocent, we must learn transgression

When violation comes,
We are split in two:
Soul lingering over Body
For years a loneliness haunts us

The pain becomes so fierce
An angel screams our name, and all hear
Lani, Angelique, Junot!
Those who named you
Pulled you out of heaven
And made you fall

Poem for My Unborn Son

an apology

Years ago yes I could have had you
You could have been born and stretched
my world around you

A life doesn't happen that way, though
Desire grows on a thought, a feeling
and extends itself, trying to grasp
what it wants

But if thoughts and feelings remain captive,
bound by debasement, poverty,
loss, coercion,
then desire doesn't form properly

It doesn't snare the light and dark,
properly braid the soft and strong,
tough and yielding
How little I understood,
myself ill formed

I had to protect you
in the non-space of being
the space of non-being
where your potential was unrealized,
unhurt by time

My perfect boy, I protected you from life

Sketch of a Father

for N.

At the beach last Sunday,
you tried to give your adolescent son a kiss.
You put your heavy arms around him,
nuzzled the down on his cheek,
and whispered,
Come on, it's natural!
But the boy was embarrassed:
he thrashed like a big fish in your arms,
then gave up,
dropped his young face into his hands.
The rest of us watched quietly,
too shy to intervene.
And you, enraged,
invoked heaven and hell in the open pavilion
like Christ at the temple,
bleating at the moneychangers
and the cold sellers of doves.

The Garden

In the dark vine climbing the flowers to the ten-pointed star
in the arch of the hands in solemn prayer

in the journey of the eye to the height of the black colonnade
in the tale of the boy who strums the harp

in the lotus shapes of the garden fountains
in the room secluded by thick Arabian curtains

in the olivine waves that crash against the rock
in the red and yellow roses broken from their stems

in the tawdry questions of the drunken man
in the tripartite name of a red-lipped girl

in the song that rouses a sleeping mind
in the nets we cast over His infinite forms

Valentine's Day 2011

Falling into dreams is the solace of poets
Burned on an altar of ragged ideas
Resting in a grave of ashes
Your oft-repeated promises
My faith,
Casual to a fault

In the immediacy of a home
A cat pushes open the door
And lets in the afternoon light
Trailing the voice of a bird
Quiet falls from the wings of the sky

The green cathedral,
The death of Father Damien
The surrender of imperial Japan
As a bird turns in flight
My hand twists in the attempt to make these lines

On a calendar known as today
In a foreign place known as the mind
I write, wondering if I still
Know the language you speak

Purple, green, and black
Make a beautiful night
Down these streets a procession of cars
A stream of grief
Lines the face of a girl

Sultry heat, they say
Characterizes summer,
But might it also be the poet's fever:

The poet wakes from a dream

It Was the Moon

It was the moon who teased me to rise
out of bed, from your side
Moonlight spilled its promise on the floor

I thought a stranger might have come through the door
but the coat of white had entered through the glass
and in our room had made itself at home

What of this encounter will you find tomorrow?
A broken camera,
disassembled into parts

and in the memory two hazy images:
a tall building and twinkling cones of light;
a shining gray cloud above a roof

No stolen kiss, no broken heart
just one witness: an ordinary poem

My Brother's Sleep

Sleep, dear brother, past the dying of the sun,
the rising of the moon

sleep till every error that holds you fast
is expelled in a sleep-filled breath

sleep as the constellations move above us
and we move toward death

sleep till there is no need for waking,
for to wake into a world of need
is not to be free

sleep, my darling:
innocence shines upon your face while you do

and I, in quiet wonder, will
watch the fiery stars for you

My Friend Looks at the Horizon

Sitting with Tom at Hau Tree Lanai,
we reach that point in a conversation
where understanding brings silence

we've been talking about the Aikaus:
Gerald, who hung himself
after stabbing his seven-year-old boy;
Eddie, who sought help for his shipmates
then was lost at sea

And I am reminded of Mahealani:
killed by her husband and then hung,
the two found side by side

Tom looks at the horizon,
beyond the mothers, children, and lovers
who claim the shore with affection
Noticing the blue perfection between ocean and sky,
he tells me of a future swim to Moloka'i,
no fanfare, no escort;
his last wishes will already be known
to his wife

The swim extends thirty miles from where we sit

under the trees on this June morning,

and when he tells me of his plan

his eyes are as fair as the sea

Friends who meet twice yearly

to talk of many things,

then the last important one:

not leaving it up to fate but choosing

the way to die

The way we might pull our bodies out of the sea

The Hunt

for K.

In dreams I hunt my sister,
follow her scent through the trees
down to the river.

                        But she is not there.

If I take this narrow trail
on the side of a mountain so steep and high
I can see a rainbow caught
in a recess of its lower slopes—
I know I will die.

                   So I make a wild and partial path

grieving
that we can't be saved.

Wading through Your Happiness

for Calvin Stewart (1952–2020)

Passing my fingers through the afternoon
the notes fall from green
to silver to gold

We are passing through the afternoon
as if for the first time:
strangers into a glowing love

Walking as if for the first time
we are touching the borders of death
the breaths

of those who went before
We will join them soon
The angle of the day

Cooling on your brow
The edge of happiness,
the nearness of death

The low notes falling from grace
I am wading through your happiness
Happy for the time being

Michelangelo Street

The silver harbor surged and scraped the air like the long skirt of a tired dancer, and the evening sky gleamed like polished brass. We were in our late twenties then: a young woman who edited a theological magazine; and a painter and a writer—two friends of her astrophysicist husband. Lorraine from a suburb and we from the Pacific, none of us knew Boston's North End, the Italian district of our destination, a restaurant known for its food. Turning from the harbor road, we soon lost our way in the umber shadows of old buildings and narrow streets. Then, certain we were far from the restaurant, impatient to begin our search, we parked beneath a tow-away sign on a dead-end street.

On a street corner three young men watched us. "If you park there, you'll lose your car for sure!" one shouted. "We live here, and they tow us away!" But Lorraine did not move her car, and the men turned away and walked up the cross street. On Michelangelo Street in the early evening, a muscular young man warned us, a young man in blue clothes and white summer shoes, his hair carefully in place as if fixed by an artist. Toward heaven the daylight departed, and the young man's hair, bones of his face, the muscles of his thighs and calves were lifted upward.

A policeman drove by on a white motorcycle, and when Lorraine stopped him and asked about the car, he stared at us, then his dark helmet bobbed and he sped away. Across the street, an old woman in a black dress stood smiling, as if we were family finally come home. Past tall brick buildings stained with the evening light and shadows, on uneven sidewalks with crushed, broken curbs, we walked. Past dirty cement courtyards where thin, gray trees grew, where Renaissance cupids, angels, young heroes defended or conquered nothing. Past figures in conversation or play—children's laughter flying like doves out of cages—past men leaning against cars, dark-haired women leaning out of windows. Under the neon lights of delis, restaurants, bakeries, we walked as if everything were waiting for us in this one place. Had we been children taken from home into a forest, we couldn't have known less about where we were going. Trash and cold air blew against our ankles, time and light loosened out of our grasp. What we passed seemed not a place but a reality antique and somber disappearing into its own shadow.

It was by accident, then, we found the restaurant on Season Street, the golden light soaking the sidewalk. And suddenly we were inside, stepping through swinging doors into a room dense with noise: patrons ordering, waiters serving cloudy white plates of pasta, vegetables, and meat. But in the steam and harsh light of the small room, we still had not found a place to rest. With no understanding of the quick talk, no names for the food or people, we ordered the most common dishes and sat like immigrants around whom the noise of the city roared.

Lorraine then asked us about our children, the Pacific, our work. With these exchanges, we tried to give each other some impression of our lives. But we could not share the most vivid details; and she seemed a young woman sitting for her portrait, her body acquiescent and contracted to the artist, the willed part of her someplace we could not reach. Had we been able to read the stillness of her eyes or the resignation of her hands, we might have known that she no longer loved her husband and would leave him within a year.

By nine when we left, the streets were dark and empty. The only light came from the moon, old street lamps, or was thrown off the dress of a young waitress as she stood in the back door of a kitchen, talking with friends. Down one street after another we walked. We followed a street we had never seen, took direction by the spire of a church white as the moon. On a dead-end street bearing the name of a great man long dead, we found a woman in black, unsmiling and wrapped tightly against the cold. The car was still there, untouched. All light and heat had returned to God. Unbound to that world, freighted with nothing but our bodies and old words, we got in the car and left Michelangelo Street.

By the Sea

If I can wholly cease to be ashamed of myself—
I think that all my days will be fair.
Emerson

Some sadness urged us along,
made our drive away from the city easy
on a summer day when rain fell at the car's back
and sent us into an afternoon without claims

to swim at Kaʻaʻawa Beach,
where you picked a lavender cloud of hyacinth
from a cold freshwater stream,
then drove us to Shark's Cove,
where we walked up a hill of old leaves, pine needles,
and heavy shadows to a beach
where children were sheltered,
growing up in the water,

then on the way back,
you turned onto Kāneʻohe Bay Drive,
showed me the sprawling house you could not,
early in your marriage, afford to buy,
then took us down a narrow road
walled by young, dark trees.

St. John's by the Sea,
you say, pointing.
That was where you sent your child,
riding your bike every morning to the small,
wooden church.
In those days, you say,
it was hard to be Caucasian. People hated you,
especially the Japanese.
Your in-laws are Japanese,
never spoke a word of English around you then,
even though, you knew,

they could speak it perfectly well.
Never even came to see their grandchild, you say.
We leave St. John's, then you say,
Look. Back there.
And I turn around to see lavender mountains
falling into a sea hammered silver by the air,
as if each is being transformed into the other,
and I hear a quiet I can't bear to leave

We stowed our hearts then, so many years ago,
sheltered in a cove where
the waters were calm and warm,
believing we could retrieve them whatever happened
however deep and many our injuries were

At O'ahu Cemetery I Saw a Lamb

resting on a black marble gravestone,
her mottled coat of brown
soaked with Nuʻuanu rain,
and out of the cavity in her back
flowed lei of orange, red, white flowers,
green leaves

the cloudburst had made a mirror
of the marble slab
and kept the flowers full and fresh
as if the soul who put them there
had just then left

the lamb, the flowers, and the gravestone
all seemed to happen in an instant
as if I'd been thinking hard about
what it is to die
and these things—unexpected and whole—
had appeared to say that death
could meet me with the face of a lamb

About the Author

Pat Matsueda is the author of *Stray*, a collection of poetry (El León Literary Arts and Mānoa Books, 2006), and *Bedeviled*, a novella (El León Literary Arts and Mānoa Books, 2017). She has been the managing editor of *Mānoa: A Pacific Journal of International Writing* since 1992 and founded the series *Ms. Aligned: Women Writing About Men* and the ezine *Vice-Versa*. She thanks Thomas Farber and Frank Stewart for their support of her writing and their friendship.

www.someperfectfuture.com